BLAZERS

The World's Deadliest

The Deadliest Bugs

on Earth

by Erika L. Shores

Reading Consultant:
Barbara J. Fox
Reading Specialist
North Carolina State University

Content Consultant:
Charles W. Fox, PhD
Professor, Department of Entomology
University of Kentucky
Lexington, Kentucky

CAPSTONE PRESS
a capstone imprint

Blazers is published by Capstone Press,
151 Good Counsel Drive, P.O. Box 669, Mankato, Minnesota 56002.
www.capstonepress.com

Library of Congress Cataloging-in-Publication Data
Shores, Erika L., 1976–
    The deadliest bugs on earth / by Erika L. Shores.
    p. cm. — (Blazers. The world's deadliest)
    Includes bibliographical references and index.
    Summary: "Describes deadly bugs and what makes them dangerous" — Provided by publisher.
    ISBN 978-1-4296-3930-9 (library binding)
    1. Insect pests — Juvenile literature. 2. Dangerous animals — Juvenile literature. 3. Poisonous
invertebrates — Juvenile literature. I. Title. II. Series: Blazers. World's deadliest.
QL468.8.S46 2010
595.7165 — dc22   2009028638

Editorial Credits

Abby Czeskleba, editor; Matt Bruning, designer; Svetlana Zhurkin, media researcher;
    Laura Manthe, production specialist

Photo Credits

Alamy/David Haynes, 27, cover (spider); Phototake/Scott Camazine, 7
CDC/James Gathany, 11, 29
Corbis/Gallo Images/Anthony Bannister, 22; Martin Harvey, 9
Getty Images/Ian Waldie, 21
iStockphoto/Mark Kostich, 5
Peter Arnold/Bios/Alain Beignet, 13; David Scharf, 25
Photolibrary/Oxford Scientific/Brian Kenney, 19; John Brown, 16
Photo Researchers/Scott Camazine, 15
Shutterstock/Alexander Potapov, cover (web); Brandon Blinkenberg, cover (wasp)

The author dedicates this book to her husband, Mike Shores, because not all bites are deadly, or
even actual bites.

TABLE OF CONTENTS

MANY-LEGGED KILLERS

Creepy, crawling, buzzing bugs can be more than backyard pests. Insects, scorpions, and spiders can kill with deadly **venom** in bites or stings.

venom – a poisonous liquid made by some bugs

SORT OF DANGEROUS

HIDDEN DANGER

Watch out for dangerous spiders like the brown recluse. The venom in this spider's bite kills **tissue**. A bite often leaves a deep hole in a person's skin.

tissue – soft material that makes up body parts

DEADLY SOLDIERS

More than 100,000 army ants march on land. Stay out of their way. Bites from army ants hurt. Bites can be deadly to people who have **allergic reactions**.

allergic reaction – an unpleasant reaction such as a rash, breathing problem, or sneezing

9

A SCARY SPIDER

The black widow is North America's most **venomous** spider. This spider's bite releases venom. People can have muscle pains and problems breathing from a black widow's bite.

DEADLY FACT

Female black widow spiders weigh 30 times more than males.

venomous – having or producing a poison called venom

Chapter 3

VERY DANGEROUS

STEALING YOUR FOOD

Locusts fly in giant swarms. They travel hundreds of miles each day. Locusts chew up and destroy crops. Without crops, people die because there isn't enough food to eat.

DEADLY FACT

Some swarms have about
100 million locusts.

BEWARE THE STING

Asian giant hornets are the world's largest hornets. They sting with sharp jabs. Allergic reactions to stings kill about 50 people a year.

DEADLY FACT

An Asian giant hornet's stinger is more than .25 inch (6.4 millimeters) long.

RUN AWAY

Africanized (AF-ri-kuh-nahyzd) honeybees are called killer bees. If bothered, these bees attack in deadly swarms. Thousands of stings from angry bees can kill.

DEADLY *FACT*

The best way to escape killer bees is to run away from them.

READY TO STING

In Africa, fat-tailed scorpions live in the cracks of walls. Fat-tailed scorpions attack with their sharp stingers. Stings from these scorpions kill more than 35 people every year.

DEADLY FACT

There are about 1,500 species of scorpions. Only 25 have deadly venom.

Chapter 4

EXTREMELY DANGEROUS

BIG FANGS

A Sydney funnel-web spider's fangs are the size of a cat's claws. The spider's fangs sink into **prey** and release venom. A person can die within one hour of being bitten.

prey – an animal hunted by another animal for food

DEADLY FACT

Male funnel-web spiders are six times more venomous than females.

YOU'RE GETTING SLEEPY

The tsetse (TSET-see) fly's bite carries an illness called sleeping sickness. People bitten by a tsetse fly suffer fevers and headaches. The illness can be deadly if people don't see a doctor.

DEADLY FACT

In Africa, 25,000 people catch sleeping sickness each year.

PUCKER UP

A bite from this bug can be the kiss of death. Kissing bugs bite near people's mouths. The bite gives them Chagas' (SHAH-guh-suz) disease. The disease causes fevers, tiredness, and sometimes death.

DEADLY FACT

Kissing bugs usually bite at night when people are sleeping.

THAT REALLY HURTS

In Brazil, people fear banana spiders. These spiders top the list of world's most venomous spiders. A painful bite causes sweating, heart problems, and even death.

TINY KILLERS

Is a mosquito really the world's deadliest bug? Yes! More than 1 million people die every year from **malaria** spread by mosquitoes. Bugs are more than just pests. And they don't have to be big to be dangerous.

malaria – a serious disease that causes high fever, chills, and sometimes death

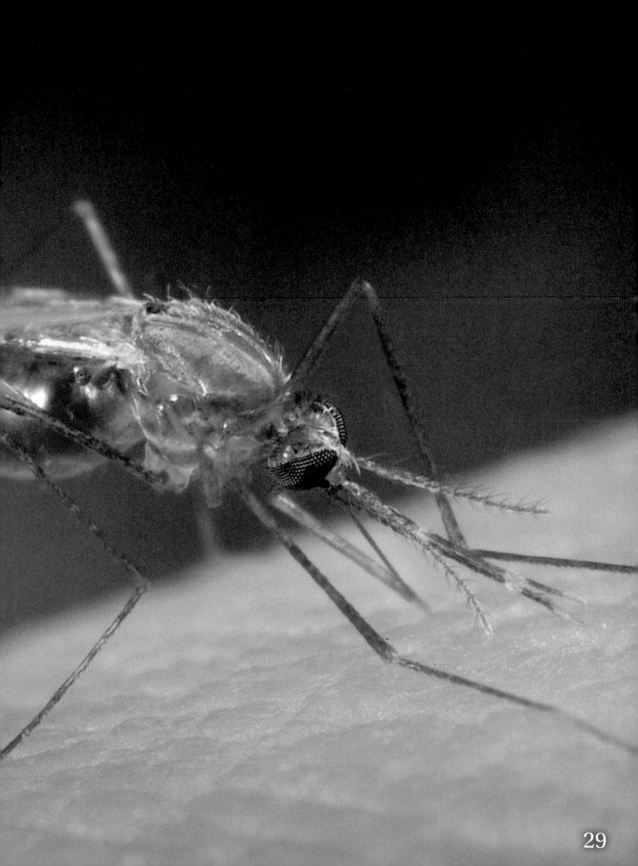

GLOSSARY

allergic reaction (uh-LUHR-jik ree-AK-shuhn) — an unpleasant reaction such as a rash, breathing problem, or sneezing

malaria (muh-LAIR-ee-ah) — a serious disease that people get from mosquito bites; malaria causes high fever, chills, and sometimes death.

prey (PRAY) — an animal hunted by another animal for food

swarm (SWORM) — a group of insects that gather and move in large numbers

tissue (TISH-yoo) — soft material that makes up body parts

venom (VEN-uhm) — a poisonous liquid made by some bugs

venomous (VEN-uh-muhss) — having or producing a poison called venom

READ MORE

Christiansen, Per. *Poisonous Spiders.* Nature's Monsters. Insects & Spiders. Pleasantville, N.Y.: Gareth Stevens, 2009.

DiConsiglio, John. *Blood Suckers!: Deadly Mosquito Bites.* 24/7. Science Behind the Scenes. New York: Franklin Watts, 2008.

Somervill, Barbara A. *Africanized Honey Bee.* 21st Century Skills Library. Animal Invaders. Ann Arbor, Mich.: Cherry Lake, 2008.

INTERNET SITES

FactHound offers a safe, fun way to find Internet sites related to this book. All of the sites on FactHound have been researched by our staff.

Here's all you do:

Visit *www.facthound.com*

FactHound will fetch the best sites for you!

INDEX